JUN 1 3

Published in 2013 by The Rosen Publishing Group, Inc.
29 East 21st Street, New York, NY 10010

Photo Credits: **KEY** tl=top left; tr=top right; cl=center left; c=center; cr=center right; bl=bottom left; bc=bottom center; br=bottom right; bg=background
CBCD = Corbis PhotoDisc; GI = Getty Images; iS = istockphoto.com; SH = Shutterstock; TF = Topfoto; wiki = Wikipedia
front cover iS; **1**c iS; **6**c iS; bc SH; **8**bl, cr wiki; **10**bl, c wiki; **12**br iS; tr wiki; **12–13**tr GI; **13**bc iS; **14**cl iS; **15**cr TF; **16**bc iS; **17**c iS; **20**tr iS; **22**bl, tl iS; **22–23**br iS; **23**cr, tl iS; **24**bc iS; **25**cl iS; br SH; **26**tr iS; **27**tl, tr iS; **28**bc iS; **30–31**bg CBCD

All illustrations copyright Weldon Owen Pty Ltd. **2–3**t, **24–25**t Inklink Studios; **6–7**c; **7**bl Andrew Davies/Creative Communication

Weldon Owen Pty Ltd
Managing Director: Kay Scarlett
Creative Director: Sue Burk
Publisher: Helen Bateman
Senior Vice President, International Sales: Stuart Laurence
Vice President Sales North America: Ellen Towell
Administration Manager, International Sales: Kristine Ravn

Library of Congress Cataloging-in-Publication Data

Park, Louise, 1961–
 Ancient cities / by Louise Park.
    p. cm. — (Discovery education: ancient civilizations)
 Includes index.
 ISBN 978-1-4777-0056-3 (library binding) — ISBN 978-1-4777-0097-6 (pbk.) —
 ISBN 978-1-4777-0098-3 (6-pack)
 1. Cities and towns, Ancient—Juvenile literature. 2. Civilization, Ancient—Juvenile literature. I. Title.
 CB311.P26 2013
 930—dc23
                            2012019577

Manufactured in the United States of America

CPSIA Compliance Information: Batch #W13PK2: For Further Information contact Rosen Publishing, New York, New York at 1-800-237-9932

ANCIENT CIVILIZATIONS

ANCIENT CITIES

LOUISE PARK

PowerKiDS
press.

New York

Contents

The Beginning of Cities

The first civilizations, or city-based cultures, developed about 5,500 years ago. The earliest of these formed in the floodplains between two rivers in a place now known as Iraq. This area is part of what is known as the Fertile Crescent, which stretches from the northern end of the Persian Gulf to the valley of the Nile River in Egypt. It was home to many ancient cities.

For ancient cities to prosper, they needed a location with access to water and other natural resources. In order to trade with other groups, they also needed access to harbors, overland trade routes, or rivers.

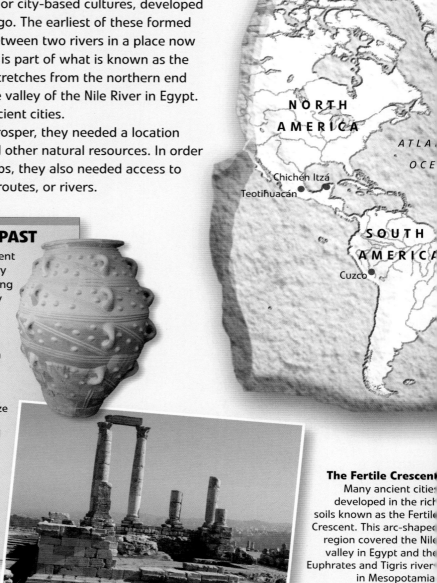

NORTH AMERICA

ATLA

OCE

Chichén Itzá
Teotihuacán

SOUTH AMERICA

Cuzco

DIGGING UP THE PAST

Archaeologists study ancient cities through the recovery of objects and by examining environmental clues. They document the past by looking at the remains of buildings, artifacts, tools, jewelry, pottery, and even the remains of people.

Pottery
Knossos is the largest Bronze Age archaeological site in Crete. Archaeologists found this pottery jar there.

City ruins
The Roman ruins in Amman, Jordan, are popular with international tourists as well as archaeologists.

The Fertile Crescent
Many ancient cities developed in the rich soils known as the Fertile Crescent. This arc-shaped region covered the Nile valley in Egypt and the Euphrates and Tigris rivers in Mesopotamia.

The word civilization comes from the Latin word civitas, *which means "city."*

Common elements

Ancient cities existed throughout Europe, Africa, the Middle East, Asia, and Central and South America. Their societies were generally organized into classes ordered by occupation—craftsmen, soldiers, merchants, priests, agricultural workers, and the ruling class. These classes shared religious beliefs and lived by the cities' rules.

THE CITY OF UR
The Fertile Crescent, Iraq

The city of Ur was located near the original mouth of the Euphrates River on the Persian Gulf in Southern Mesopotamia. It was one of many small cities settled by a people known as Sumerians. By 2100 BC, Ur had taken over as the most important city in Mesopotamia. Some archaeologists believe that, at its peak, Ur was the largest city in the world. Its population is thought to have been between 30,000 and 65,000 people.

As the city grew, Ur's kings became the rulers of the entire Kingdom of Sumeria. Elaborate tombs were built for the city's kings and queens, and held many treasures. Several spectacular temples and monuments were also built.

Cuneiform
This highly developed early writing system used abstract symbols made of wedge-shaped marks. These were pressed into a clay tablet with a stylus made of reed. The wet clay was then baked or left to dry.

Statue to the gods
The people of Ur worshipped many gods and built temples in their honor. This statue of a worshipper was found inside one of the temples.

Babylon

Ancient Babylon was one of the most advanced city-states in Mesopotamia. The Babylonians developed early forms of economics, astronomy, medicine, agriculture, mathematics, and philosophy. Their system for measuring time, using units of 60 seconds and 60 minutes, is still used.

The arch
The invention of the archway allowed Mesopotamians to build larger and grander buildings.

Glazed bricks
The Babylonians brushed bricks with a paste before baking them to create shiny, colored surfaces.

Religious symbols
Mesopotamian gods were molded onto bricks during the brickmaking process for protection and worship.

THE CITY OF MOHENJO DARO
The Indus Valley, Pakistan

The first attempts at building cities in the Indian subcontinent were in the Indus Valley. This valley had a good river and decent annual rainfall, which meant that crops grew easily and cities, such as Mohenjo Daro, could thrive. Built in 2500 BC, Mohenjo Daro had planned streets with big public buildings, workers' quarters, and houses all built with bricks that were baked in wood-fired ovens. The city housed around 40,000 people, and their homes had bathrooms that connected to sewers and water pipes.

The people of the Indus Valley were the first to make fabric from cotton. They also had a writing system based on pictographs, and used a system of weights and measures. The ruins of Mohenjo Daro were discovered in the 1920s in what is Pakistan today.

Highly skilled
The people of the Indus Valley were skilled with their hands. They made knives, bowls, and weapons from bronze. They also made toys, such as this wheeled animal.

Priest King
This statue was discovered in 1927 by archaeologists who named it the Priest King. It is thought to be a statue of a ruler or priest.

Public baths

Excavated in the 1920s, the Great Baths of Mohenjo Daro represent the world's earliest communal water-holding structure. Water was supplied from a large well and could be emptied via a large drain. The baths measured 897 square feet (83 m²).

Easy access
Wide, wooden staircases at the north and south ends led into the water.

Ritual bathing
The bath was nearly 10 feet (3 m) deep and almost 40 feet (12 m) long. Historians believe the complex was used to purify and renew the well-being of believers.

No leaking
Finely fitted mud-brick tiles were covered with a tarlike substance to make the bath watertight.

Air-conditioning
The wooden roof reflected the Sun and kept the baths cool.

THE CITY OF KNOSSOS

The Minoans of Crete, Greece

Mainland Greece was close to the Fertile Crescent and home to the Minoans, who lived there from around 2500 BC. The civilization was at its greatest between 2200 and 1450 BC. The people built elaborate towns that each had a palace as the focus.

Knossos was one of the Minoans' largest cities, and the remains of its palace were discovered more than 100 years ago. Often referred to as the Labyrinth, the palace had a large, central square that connected to a maze of workrooms, storerooms, and living spaces. It had more than 1,000 rooms in total. Knossos is located near the ancient city of Heraklion, and is thought to have been the center of ceremonial and political Minoan civilization and culture.

Labrys ax
A double-headed ax called a *labrys* symbolized the mother goddess of all Minoan culture. Many paintings of this symbol exist throughout the palace in Knossos.

Reconstructed ruins
After Sir Arthur Evans, a British archaeologist, unearthed and bought the Knossos palace site, he assembled a team to reconstruct and restore it. He did not always use authentic materials and many frescoes were created from just a tiny fragment of remaining art.

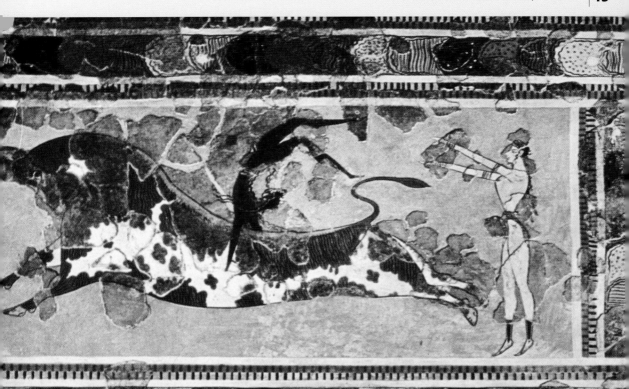

Unreconstructed ruins
Much of the city of Knossos has been left in its original state to preserve its history. Some scholars have argued that by reconstructing modern additions over the ruins, Sir Arthur Evans has caused damage.

Frescoes
The Knossos palace walls were decorated with frescoes depicting scenes at court. The most famous is the Toreador fresco, which depicts a man somersaulting over a bull.

Did You Know?
British archaeologist Sir Arthur Evans named the Minoans for King Minos, who is said to have lived on Crete. We do not know what the Minoans called themselves.

THE CITY OF ATHENS
Monuments to the Gods, Greece

At its peak, Athens had a population of between 50,000 and 100,000, and was one of the most powerful of all the city-states. The birthplace of democracy, many consider it to be at the center of the cradle of civilization.

Athens thrived on trade, agriculture, crafts, and wealth. It invested in the education of its people and allowed for philosophy, literature, architecture, mathematics, and democracy to be explored and developed. The philosopher Socrates, the playwright Sophocles, and the politician Themistocles were all Athenians.

The Parthenon
Completed in 437 BC, the Parthenon was built on a hill overlooking the city of Athens, over the ruins of a temple razed during the Persian invasion. The Parthenon was dedicated to the goddess Athena, who, the people believed, protected their city.

Goddess Athena
A statue of the goddess Athena stood in one of the rooms.

Tourist attraction
The Parthenon today stands in modern Athens as a monument to the ancient city-state. Some sections have been restored, but most of the original building still stands.

GREEK COLUMNS

Doric, Ionic, and Corinthian orders are styles of columns used in Greek architecture. The Parthenon was mainly a Doric temple. It was surrounded by Doric columns and had four Ionic columns inside.

Doric order

Ionic order

Corinthian order

Carved stone
Painted sculptures told stories from Greek mythology that related to Athens.

Socrates
Considered to be the father of Western philosophy, Socrates was one of the first people to apply logic and reason to everyday living.

THE CITY OF PETRA
City of Rocks, Jordan

Petra sat at the crossroads of a number of ancient trade routes. Carved out of sandstone and with a good supply of water, it became the capital city of the Nabataean people. For nearly 500 years, these people controlled one of the most important trade routes.

The main route into this mountain stronghold was from the east. Travelers approached along a narrow gorge of towering sandstone that was between only 10 and 13 feet (3 and 4 m) wide in some places. The pathway was about 1.25 miles (2 km) long, with the sandstone walls reaching 200 feet (60 m) high in some places. The end of this narrow pass opened to a terrace and the city itself.

Did You Know?
Certain sites at Petra, most notably the Treasury, were used as locations in the film *Indiana Jones and the Last Crusade*. Petra also appears in the film *Transformers: Revenge of the Fallen*.

Petra unearthed
An explorer rediscovered Petra in 1812. Despite many years of excavation since then, archaeologists believe only a tiny fraction of the city has been unearthed.

The Treasury

Probably the most well-known site at Petra is the "Treasury of the Pharaohs." It is the first thing visitors see when arriving at the end of the narrow gorge known as the Sik. The Greek facade, with its columns carved directly from the cliff face, is about 98 feet (30 m) high. Despite its name, it bears no relation to the Pharaohs of Egypt and was never used as a treasury. It was, in fact, an unfinished tomb facade.

THE CITY OF CHANG'AN
Million People's City, China

The city of Chang'an sat on a fertile plain known as Guanzhong in northwest China. For 200 years, between AD 700 and 900, it was one of the most sophisticated cities of its time. The imperial city was built first, followed by the outer city. The streets were laid out in a mathematical grid, with commercial and private areas separated. There were stores, restaurants, and active business centers pulsing with traveling merchants, foreign traders, scholars, and other visitors.

Located on the famous Silk Road, Chang'an was the political, economic, and cultural center of China. The people of Chang'an mass-produced commodities such as farming tools, silk cloth, and paper. This gave the emperors control over the whole eastern end of the Silk Road, which linked Asia and Europe.

Water families
Some families lived on houseboats. Babies often had bamboo floats tied to their back to protect them from drowning.

DRESSED FOR STATUS

Clothing was a sign of class in ancient China. The texture, color, and decoration indicated the wearer's position in society. Fine silk, for example, was reserved for high-ranking officials.

Women's dress
Women wore a long skirt and jacket, topped by a short-sleeved upper garment. They also wore powder and makeup.

The emperor's clothes
Yellow was considered the highest-ranking color, so only the emperor wore yellow clothes.

Men's dress
Men generally wore loose robes and hats. Wide sleeves were weighted so they could hang without flapping.

Horse and cart
Officials traveled by horse and cart. Some were even buried with them so they would not have to walk in the afterlife.

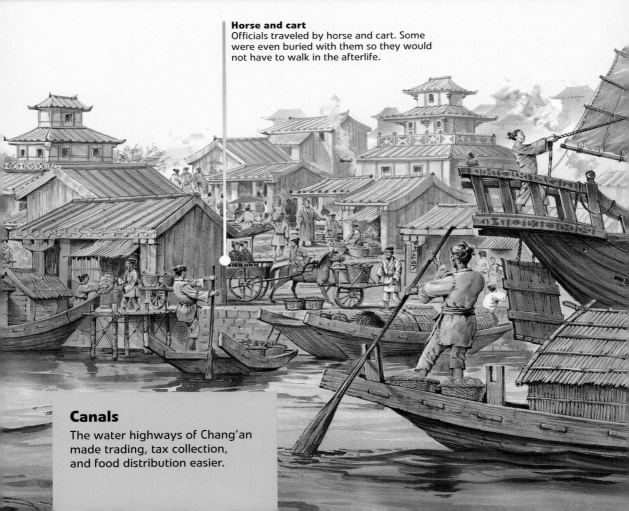

Canals
The water highways of Chang'an made trading, tax collection, and food distribution easier.

City of Pyramids, Mexico

Chichén Itzá was built by the Mayan civilization near the northern tip of the Yucatán Peninsula of present day Mexico. The city became a religious center of importance between AD 625 and 800 and quickly rose to the status of a capital city. During its almost 1,000-year history, it dominated political and social life in the northern Mayan lowlands.

The Mayan people were skilled farmers, traders, and builders. Their sophisticated civilization ran on a class system, and they used what is thought be the first written language native to Americans.

Chichén Itzá ruins
The ruins of highly decorated temple-pyramids, palaces, and observatories are testimony to the advanced building skills of the Maya.

Human sacrifice
Humans and gold treasures were thrown into large wells as an act of sacrifice. The Maya believed sacrifices to the gods would keep them safe from drought and famine.

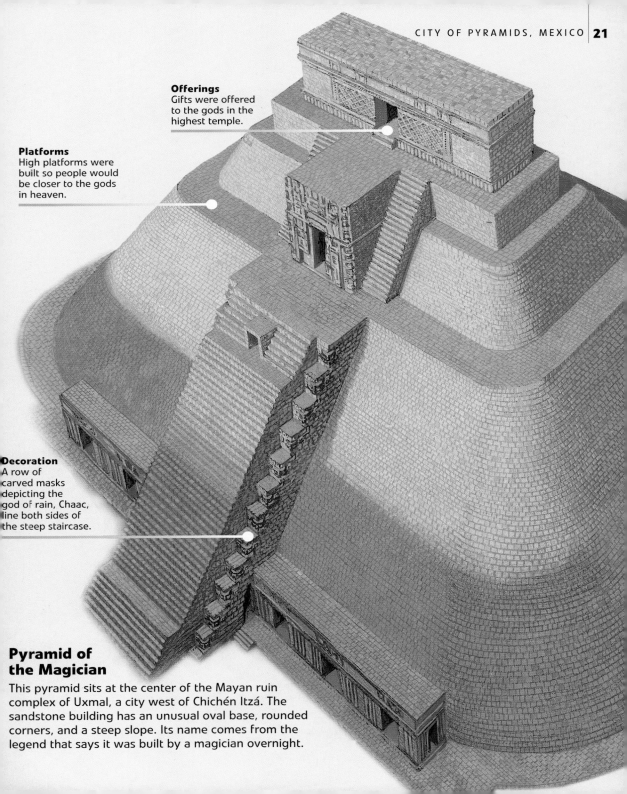

Offerings
Gifts were offered
to the gods in the
highest temple.

Platforms
High platforms were
built so people would
be closer to the gods
in heaven.

Decoration
A row of
carved masks
depicting the
god of rain, Chaac,
line both sides of
the steep staircase.

Pyramid of the Magician

This pyramid sits at the center of the Mayan ruin
complex of Uxmal, a city west of Chichén Itzá. The
sandstone building has an unusual oval base, rounded
corners, and a steep slope. Its name comes from the
legend that says it was built by a magician overnight.

Intricate work
A carving of a kala, a mythical creature that represented time, and the god Shiva can be found in the Banteay Srei temple at Angkor.

THE CITY OF ANGKOR
City of Temples, Cambodia

Angkor is located in modern day Cambodia. It was originally the center of the Khmer Empire, which reached its peak between the ninth and fifteenth centuries. More than 1,000 extraordinary stone temples built during that time still exist, and the area is now known as the city of temples.

Among the Angkor religious sites sits Angkor Wat, the southernmost temple, and the most renowned. It is the world's largest religious monument.

Trees on the ruins
Large trees and tree roots have grown over the temple ruins over the last 200 years. These are holding some of the crumbling sandstone walls together.

Welcome path

The causeway leading toward Angkor Thom, north of Angkor Wat, is lined with 54 statues of gods on one side and 54 statues of demons on the other side.

The Bayon temple

At the center of Angkor Thom lies the Bayon temple. This is famous for its huge stone faces that jut out from the towers of the terrace.

Angkor Wat

The huge temple known as Angkor Wat was built during the twelfth century. Its original architecture was very detailed for its time, with ceiling panels and doors made from carved wood. The temple itself consists of three rectangular areas, each higher than the other, that build up to the main tower. The moat surrounding the temple is 625 feet (190 m) wide.

THE CITY OF CUZCO

Mysterious Master Masons, Peru

Legend has it that the city of Cuzco was founded by the great leader of Incan civilization, Sapa Inca Pachacuti. The original city was built in the Andes mountains of Peru, around AD 1300, and many important buildings were rebuilt in stone in 1438.

During the fifteenth century, Cuzco became the Inca capital. It was a religious and governmental city with very few residential buildings. Its four main streets led to the four districts, or provinces, of the Inca empire. These were run by four governors who met with the emperor in Cuzco every year.

Machu Picchu
Although no one knows for sure, this citadel was thought to have been built for the Inca leader Sapa Inca Pachacuti. Located high in the Andes mountains, northwest of Cuzco, the ruins include terraced gardens down the mountainside.

Hard at work

Everyone in the Incan population, including children, worked hard. Women and men had equal tasks, and work ranged from pottery and masonry to weaving and tapestry-making.

Record–keeping

The Incans used knots to record information. The knots were distinguished by their color and position on the string.

Masonry

can masonry work was very dvanced for its time. Large ones were cut and shaped so recisely, they could fit together ghtly without mortar.

e Sun god

e Incans
rshipped the
god, Inti.
un mask was
g in temples
people prayed
for good weather
healthy crops.

THE CITY OF TEOTIHUACÁN

Empire of the Sun, Mexico

Teotihuacán sat in the Valley of Mexico, and was first settled in about 150 BC. It was not until the first century AD, however, that it developed into a city. The center was carefully laid out, with avenues crossing each other and meeting in a great compound that was the marketplace.

By around AD 500, the city had a population of 200,000 that included master potters, jewelers, and craftsmen. Its workers irrigated the Teotihuacán Valley, quarried stone, grew crops, and owned livestock.

Stone calendar
Many believed this stone to be a calendar. It shows carvings of the names of the days and the cosmogenic Suns on it.

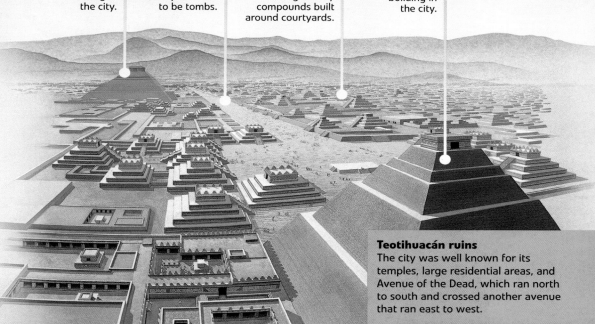

Sun pyramid
This pyramid was the largest building in the city.

Avenue of the Dead
This held what many believed to be tombs.

Residential complexes
Most families lived in single-story compounds built around courtyards.

Moon pyramid
This was the second largest building in the city.

Teotihuacán ruins
The city was well known for its temples, large residential areas, and Avenue of the Dead, which ran north to south and crossed another avenue that ran east to west.

Masks
Often depicting gods, these masks were used for sacrificial and ceremonial purposes.

Skull wall
Many Mesoamerican civilizations used skull racks to display the remains of war captives or sacrificial bones.

Shield
Chimalli was a shield carried by warriors. Some, like this one, were decorative.

Armor
Ichcahuipilli was quilted cotton armor that was resistant to swords.

Club
Huitzauhqui was a wooden club with sharp blades down each side.

Aztec warrior
The Aztecs, who lived in Mexico in later centuries, were heavily influenced by Teotihuacán culture. All young Aztec men trained as soldiers and they often sacrificed their war prisoners to the gods. Soldiers who took many prisoners wore elaborate uniforms.

THE CITY OF TIMBUKTU

Fabled City of Learning, Africa

That's Amazing!
Camels can travel up to 25 miles (40 km) a day without needing to stop for food and water. They use energy from the lump of fat that is stored in their hump.

Nomads founded Timbuktu during the twelfth century near the edge of the Niger River in Africa, and it grew to be one of the major trading ports for the caravans in the Sahara desert. From the early 1200s to the 1500s, Timbuktu was one of the richest towns in Africa. The city's merchants traded gold, ivory, cola nuts, and slaves to foreign traders who exchanged salt, cloth, copper, and food goods.

Being close to the river, miners of salt would carry it into Timbuktu, where merchants would then transport it on the river to other places. Primarily known as a trading city, Timbuktu slowly became known for its religious and educational wealth. The city was destroyed by the war between Morocco and Songhai, and only a small version of it remains.

Djenné mosque
About 220 miles (350 km) southwest of Timbuktu lies the Djenné mosque, the largest mud-brick structure in the world. Built sometime between the twelfth and thirteenth centuries, it was made with sun-baked mud bricks and a mud-based mortar, then covered with a mud plaster to provide a smooth finish.

Tuareg bandits

The Sahara is the largest desert in the world and traders crossed it on camels. Crossing the Sahara was not easy. Many traders were attacked by Tuareg tribesmen from surrounding areas. They wore veiled turbans and robbed traders of their goods.

Glossary

Bronze Age (BRONZ AYJ)
The period between 3300 and 1200 BC, when cultures adopted the use of bronze for metalworking.

causeway (KAHZ-way)
A raised path or track over wet or low ground.

citadel (SIT-ah-del)
A fortress that protects a city or town.

commodities (kuh-MAH-duh-teez)
Raw materials, crops, or agricultural products that can be bought or sold.

compound (KOM-pownd)
Something that is composed of two or more separate elements.

cosmogenic (koz-muh-JEH-nik)
Relating to evolution or the universe.

democracy (dih-MAH-kruh-see)
A system of government by a whole population that strives for the principles of social equality.

famine (FA-men)
An extreme lack of food.

floodplains (FLUD-playnz)
Flat or nearly flat land near a river or lake that experiences periodic flooding.

gorge (GORJ)
A narrow valley between mountains or hills.

imperial (im-PEER-ee-ul)
Relating to an empire or emperor.

irrigated (IR-uh-gayt-ed)
Supplied and channeled water that helps crops grow.

lowlands (LOH-landz)
Low-lying areas of a country.

monument (MON-yuh-mint) A building, structure, or site of historical importance.

mortar (MOR-tur)
A paste that sets hard and is used to bind construction blocks together.

philosophy (feh-LAH-suh-fee)
The study of reality, existence, knowledge, and thinking.

:rifice (SA-kruh-fys)
killing of an animal or person
n offering to the gods.

subcontinent
(sub-KON-tin-ent)
A large and recognizable
part of a continent.

lus (STY-lis)
nall rod with a pointed end
is used for scratching
kings into clay.

treasury (TREH-zher-ee)
The place where the funds of a
society or government are kept.

Index

Websites

Due to the changing nature of Internet links, PowerKids Press has developed an online list of websites related to the subject of this book. This site is updated regularly. Please use this link to access the list: www.powerkidslinks.com/disc/anci/